Spark of Brilliance

Poems by Children

Volume 1

First published in Great Britain in 2022
by Spark of Brilliance
an imprint of Book Brilliance Publishing
265A Fir Tree Road, Epsom, Surrey, KT17 3LF
+44 (0)20 8641 5090
www.bookbrilliancepublishing.com
admin@bookbrilliancepublishing.com

Copyright © Brenda Dempsey 2022
Cover design and additional images (pages 17, 29, 37)
by Tammy Clark at Art by T Clark

The moral right of Brenda Dempsey to be identified as
the author of this work has been asserted in accordance
with the Copyright, Designs and Patents Acts 1988.

All rights reserved. No part of this publication
may be reproduced, stored in a retrieval system,
or transmitted, in any form or by any means without
the prior written permission of the publisher,
nor be otherwise circulated in any form of binding
or cover than that in which it is published
and without similar condition being imposed
on the subsequent purchaser.

A CIP catalogue record for this book
is available at the British Library.

ISBN 978-1-913770-41-9
Printed by 4edge Ltd

Dedicated to all of the Sparks of Brilliance
who shared their poems.

Contents

Introduction by Brenda Dempsey	9
A Note from the Editor	13

The Top Three — 15

My Family of Gods by Lucas Jobson	16
An Ode to Autumn by Aaryn Padhi	18
The Two Sides of Autumn by Beatrice Pollard	20

Certificate of Excellence — 23

Space by Rachel Pennington	24
Awesome Autumn by Risheet Mandal	26
Dave on the Sun by Coco Coombes	28
Space Voyage by Rachel Antony	30
Awesome Autumn by Lucy King	32
The Rickety Rackety Railway by Sujay Gundala	34

My Family by Holly Edwards	36
Stargazing by Jack Lewis	38
The Optimist by Vio Boldizsar	40

Certificate of Achievement 41

Autumn's Love by Faaezah Ahmed Shaik	43
The Two Little Lost Puppies by Saanvi Tadikamalla	44
Autumn by Keya Patel	46
Spectacular Space by Sairithvika Mallina	48
Stars by Aarav Bibin Bhanu	50
Fluffy, My Magic Puppy! by Adya Gupta Ram	51
My Dream Place by Harshika Yeleswarapu	52
Autumn by Nikola Diakomanolis	53
All the Way to the Moon by Shon Paul	54
Autumn by Athusga Dineshkumar	55

Autumn Poem by Aamna Ahmed	56
From the Darkness by Phoenix Kilgour	57
Feeling Autumn by Keera Bates	58
Autumn by Hiruki Tennakoon	60
Dying to Live a Many More by Rosy Ilieva	61
Autumn by Bumiga Barathethas	62
The Solar System and Space by Kayla Osileye	64
Flowers by Joanna Idowu	66
Acknowledgements & Sponsors	67

Introduction
by Brenda Dempsey

Every child is a natural born writer.

It's a privilege being a publisher. It's a joy being a teacher. When you combine these two jobs, you create magic for both writer and reader.

My name is Brenda Dempsey, CEO of Book Brilliance Publishing in Surrey. As an educational specialist with 25 years' teaching experience, I know the importance of giving our children wider opportunities beyond the classroom. It is vital that children see the connection between their classroom learning and the real world.

Our children have undergone an unprecedented challenge in the past few years. Book Brilliance Publishing champions young authors and promotes Diversity and Inclusion. We are mindful of the effect the recent pandemic has had on our children's mental well-being and are excited to launch our inaugural children's poetry book born out of our first competition, Spark of Brilliance.

Our intention was to ignite motivation, boost confidence, and show the children that they have something significant to offer others.

Our mission was to raise future voices and offer our children the opportunity to do that through poetry. As a teacher, it was my favourite aspect of language that I loved to share with the children.

Out of this, Spark of Brilliance was born. We also wanted to develop closer working relationships with the young people and schools in our community, so we began right here in Epsom and surrounding towns in Surrey.

I was very excited because I have loved poetry since I was a child. The rhyme, rhythm and words that dance in your mouth as you read them aloud thrill me in a way that reaches my soul.

After reaching out to many of the local Surrey schools, we found ourselves joyfully reading through a ton of poetry. We had presented the children with six themes: space, autumn, my family, my pet, my school, and my favourite place.

What a challenge it was trying to find a winner! We wanted a broad spectrum within the judging panel so we invited a young poetry competition finalist, as well as a writer, TV presenter and grandfather, along with the Book Brilliance Publishing team to judge these wonderful, expressive poems.

As a publisher, we work with great illustrators, so Book Brilliance Publishing's illustrator Tammy Clark agreed to create the front cover which was part of the prize for the winner. The cover of the book you now hold in your hands is based on the winning poem, *My Family of Gods* by Lucas Jobson from All Saints Benhilton C of E Primary School, Sutton. His poem reflected his family as gods so we knew the front cover would be a hit and, of course, it had to have stars on it, just like all the children who entered the competition.

Ordering the poems as finalists was another very challenging task so we decided to pick our top ten, which soon became our top twelve, and from that we selected the top three poems. On another day and with different judges, the top twelve could be different; however, the winning poem did stand out for us.

Apart from the first, second and third prize-winning poems, the other poems in each section of this book are listed in no particular order.

Poetry is a wonderful way to express thoughts, ideas and emotions. You often hear the phrase 'poetic licence'. This is the term used to describe that writing conventions are sometimes bent for effect within poetry. You may see evidence of this in some of the poems in the way that they are written, sentence structure and punctuation.

This book is Volume 1 which suggests we will be repeating this competition, not just here in Surrey but other counties surrounding it. We have joined with an organisation from Kent, Education Life CIC, whose mission it is to report and spread good news, so we hope they may be able to help us in the future.

It is our intention to support the BookTrust so that no child is deprived of reading, as we feel reading allows their imagination to blossom. Therefore, £1 from each copy of this book that is purchased will be donated to the BookTrust.

> You can find magic
> wherever you look.
> Sit back and relax
> all you need is a book.
>
> Dr Seuss

Brenda Dempsey
CEO
Book Brilliance Publishing

A Note from the Editor
by Olivia Eisinger

☆

Welcome to Book Brilliance Publishing's inaugural Spark of Brilliance poetry book – poems written by local primary school children in Years 5 and 6.

When we launched the competition in September 2021, we had no idea what to expect – how many submissions we would receive, or what sort of poems children wanted to write. The past two years have been tough on everyone, including primary school children who have missed their friends and the social routine of a classroom, as well as having to learn in a completely different way to how children normally learn. We wanted to give children a wider opportunity beyond the classroom and do something to help their well-being and restore their confidence – and what better way to do this than through poetry?

We gave the children six subjects to choose from: space, autumn, my family, my pet, my school and my favourite place. To say we were blown away by the standard of the poems submitted is an understatement. We could not believe the breadth of ideas, poetic techniques, feelings and emotions, but, above all, IMAGINATION that we received. Thirty wonderful finalists are featured in this book, with the outstanding winning poem, *My Family of Gods* by Lucas Jobson, being represented on the cover.

Thank you again to all the children who submitted poems and well done again to our finalists and our top three!

Olivia Eisinger
Editor
Book Brilliance Publishing

The Top Three

First Place

My Family of Gods
by Lucas Jobson

Zeus is in Olympus,
Poseidon in the sea.
Hades in the Underworld,
Apollo's above me.

Artemis is hunting,
Athena's out at war.
Iris in the rainbows,
Demeter's growing more.

Hephaestus forging for the Gods,
Dionysus drinking wine.
Hermes winging messages,
Ares on the battle line.

I'm rather keen on Greek myths,
Recalling all the facts.
I see their different qualities,
In my family and their acts.

My dad is like Zeus,
He's the God of the sky.
Always stuck upstairs,
Working to pay our water supply.

Which is needed for Poseidon,
My brother if you will.
Who spends hours swimming lengths,
An equal distance to Brazil.

My mother is like Athena,
She always has a plan.
Sharing strategies and wisdom,
To make me a good man.

I live with two more members,
Female goddesses, strong and brave.
These two fierce young ladies,
Match the way we behave.

I'd compare my aunt to Persephone,
Goddess of the seasons.
She is good at growing plants,
For many different reasons.

The smallest one I've got for you,
Let's call her Nemesis in here.
She's always plotting her revenge,
My sister's one to fear!

Second Place

An Ode to Autumn
by Aaryn Padhi

Leaves pirouette like dancing stars,
Reds, oranges and yellow gold bars,
The buzz of the harvester is loud and clear.
The tweet of bird fills my ear,
As well as the rustle of the leaves I hear.

Bare trees wave in the blustery breeze,
In the cold weather next season,
the water will freeze.
Pumpkins grin with an eerie light,
The shine of the sun is no longer bright.

The sun frowns as its heat is over,
The shower beats down upon the clover.
Shimmering fireworks light up the starry sky,
Autumn is here as summer says goodbye.

A poppy gravely bows its red head,
Out of respect for the brave, now dead.
Conkers fall with a plop,
Squirrels wait patiently for the nuts
the trees will drop.

Summer is a jet flying by,
Causing tears in my eye.
Never fear! It will be back.
Now, we need to follow autumn's track.

Third Place

Two Sides of Autumn
by Beatrice Pollard

The cool and gentle breeze,
Amber and brown autumnal leaves,
Beauty far beyond one's eye can see,
Stunning colours, rich, wealthy,
Autumn is part of nature's cure,
Can you deny his persuading lure?
Birds of pure peace soaring high in the sky,
Tears of rain, clouds that cry.
The wind starts smooth
but then gets powerfully scary.
Another side of autumn now we see.

Full of rage and a desire to kill,
Do what he wants,
He can and he will.
Fast freezing rain and gales of wind.

Wind of pain,
Dead leaves falling to the floor,
Can the world take anymore?
Shadows of autumn filled the night,
Shadows of autumn fill hearts with fright.
The calling is no longer tame,
The luring is no longer sane.

But with this hatred comes a delicate beauty.
Although he is a frightening enemy,
An amazing friend it can be.
Trees gnarled tall and proud,
Howling wind confident and loud.
Let autumn embrace you
and run through your blood,
You'll know what to do.

Certificate of Excellence

⭐

Space
by Rachel Pennington

I look up to the sky,
And see a rocket flying by,
I look up to the ship,
And see it do a flip,
I wish I could fly
Into that shadowed sky.

Spectacular,
Powerful,
Amazing,
Cool and,
Exciting.

As dark as night,
It is my delight,
A vortex of mystery,
Adventure through history.

Spectacular,
Powerful,
Amazing,
Cool and,
Exciting.

A myriad of stars,
Shimmer in the sky,
I can even see Mars,
When I peer up really high.

Spectacular,
Powerful,
Amazing,
Cool and,
Exciting.

Space is a marvel,
Space is a vortex of time,
Space is my delight.

A shadowy blanket envelopes me,
More crushing than the depths of the sea.
That is space.

Awesome Autumn
by Risheet Mandal

Rain replaces the sun as autumn has begun!
Pitter-pattering on the window pane,
Sending water to us once again.
Colour and beauty among the leaves,
Creating a sight that almost nobody believes.

Red, orange and yellow hue,
gives us a spectacular view
The nature looks so merry;
it feels like a land of fairy.
Crunching satisfyingly beneath our feet,
Leaves cover the grassy ground,
Like the fur on an enormous Afghan hound.

Halloween ghosts start to be seen,
Pumpkins soon appear looking all very mean.
Children wear costumes as they trick or treat,
Are they looking for candy or a spooky greet?

The farmers becomes very busy
as the harvest start,
Collecting strawberries, apples,
and cabbages is one big part.

Soon, coldness starts to bite
and bears start to say goodnight!
Creatures big and small start to hibernate,
As temperatures grow low at an amazing rate.

Then the rain turns to snow
as winter starts to grow,
Lakes start to freeze,
and colder turns the breeze.

Dave on the Sun
by Coco Coombes

Have you once heard,
Of a cow with long legs?
And ears as thin,
As the thinnest of pegs?

Well I'll show you him,
He lives up there!
And relaxes in the night,
Without a care!

His name is Dave,
And he's very brave,
For once he fought in animal war,
And helped his pet dog with a hurt paw!

Dave has exceptionally good taste,
And his smile, oh his *smile*!
His smile is so enlightening,
It could easily travel more than a mile!

Dave's pet dog is called Steve-Pete,
And after Steve-Pete's daily swim,
He goes off to relax in the heat!

Have you once heard,
Of a cow with long legs?
And ears as thin,
As the thinnest of pegs?

Well here's something true,
Now you do!

Space Voyage
by Rachel Antony

10, 9, 8, 7, 6, 5, 4, 3, 2, 1!
Blast off to space, not to the sun,
let's have fun!

We're in the sky,
Way up high,
Starting to fly.

It's wondrous,
Mysterious,
Even cryptic,
Like an artist's work: artistic.
All the planets whirling around the star,
Looking at the closest planet, yet so far.

Awestruck at the sight of Earth:
a glass blue bead,
Staring, glaring, very good indeed.
All the stars like diamonds sparkling,
Me, jaw-dropped, as I was stargazing,

The sun beamed at me,
As I looked down to see,
A whole solar system, getting dizzy.

A radio said I had to come back to them,
I was sad; my space trip had come to an end,
But I could come back again!

Awesome Autumn
by Lucy King

Out and about feeling chilly,
the autumn wind makes us act silly.

Coats on zzzzziiiipppppp,
to the park quick!

Under the tree leaves pile red and gold,
squirrels bury their nuts ready for the cold.

Muddy wellies, muddy puddles,
frothy hot chocolate with lots of bubbles.

Pumpkins are picked and ready to light,
tables filled with yummy delight!

Knock knock, trick or treat,
don't be scared, just take a sweet!

Now clocks go back in time,
snoozing for an hour feels sublime!

Remember, remember the 5th of November,
before we know it will be December.

People gathering to see the bright lights,
it's exciting to be allowed out at night.

Whizz, crackle, pop, boom,
fireworks exploding sparkling with the moon.

Now it's nearly Christmas break,
with family and presents, I just can't wait!

There may not be so much sun,
but now it's autumn, let's have fun!

The Rickety Rackety Railway
by Sujay Gundala

With a hush and a hoot,
And a brush and a toot,
Never stopping,
And never starting,
And laying still like dead troops,
The carriage following but nobody knows,
To nowhere it seems, away it goes!

Slower than snails, slower than sloths,
Driver and passengers, nowhere to be seen,
Sitting and moaning, like it's never been,
Running along, like it should have been.

Moaning and groaning, huffing and puffing,
Now it seems the end is near,
Desperate in need for a person in need,
Crying along to the mocking wind,
Being abandoned from what it loves,
Never once around the coves.

Blacker than black, the tears dropped by,
The end is near and it knew it well,
It used its might to hold on,
But this tale is not bold as told,
As the rickety rackety railway train,
Trembled to the ground.

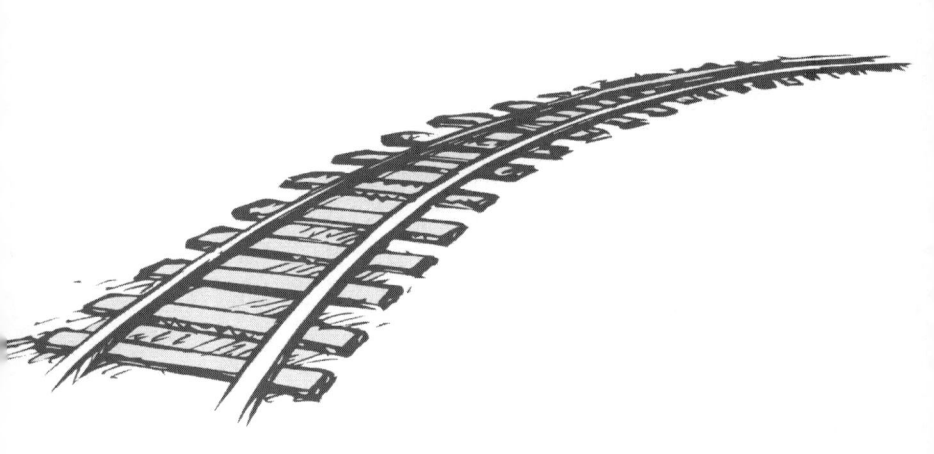

My Family
by Holly Edwards

Me and my family,
A family of four,
Buckle up and get ready,
I'm opening the door.

I'll start with Amy,
She's my sister,
She laughs and giggles,
I really miss her.

Next is my mum,
She is fun and jolly,
She is there for me,
Although she can be a wally.

Then it's my dad,
He makes me laugh,
He loves football,
I'm not daft.

Finally it's me,
I'm here right now,
All in my own world,
Taking a bow.

So this is my family,
A family of four,
So calm down now,
I'm closing the door.

Stargazing
by Jack Lewis

As I gaze upon the starlit sky,
I watch the comets fizzing by.
The silence echoes in my ears,
Banishing my inside fears.

The moon and the stars shine from above,
Showing what I dearly love.
Each planet that hangs up on high,
Shows you the beauty of the sky.

The man who hides there, in the moon,
Will soon hide his face from view.
In Earth's orbit, flying round,
The ISS beats every sound.

The moon shines down and lights me up,
Each dial on my telescope.
A glimmer rises from the ground,
There was a light; a new day was bound.

The golden orb peeks over the hill,
As I know it always will.
A fiery orange shines along,
And glows beside the blackbird's song.

The sunrise starts, a wondrous sight,
And all the birds begin their flight.

The Optimist
by Vio Boldizsar

They found a little courage,
That shimmered in the sun,
It blended in with patience,
And just a spice of fun.

They poured in hope and laughter,
And with a sudden twist…
They stirred it all together,
And made an optimist.

Imagine…
They found it way too timorous,
Or too downhearted to light up the clouds.
It was meant to avoid big dreams,
It was made of depression and anxiety,
That reinforced the lack of hope and joy…

And guess what they've done?
They stirred it all together,
And made a pessimist.

Certificate of Achievement

Autumn's Love
by Faaezah Ahmed Shaik

I always will love autumn,
as it is filled with optimism.
The beautiful crispy, golden leaves,
fall elegantly from the trees.

The birds gracefully sing:
Ting! Ting! Ting!
They sing with melody,
never with melancholy.

There are delicious sweets,
and mouth-watering treats.
It's Halloween season!

As autumn kisses goodbye,
Christmas says hi.
Christmas light greets,
in the silent streets.

The Two Little Lost Puppies
by Saanvi Tadikamalla

Two little lost puppies, one stormy night,
Lost in the dark, with no light in sight,
Drenched and starving,
searching for their mum,
Their paws numb, and spirits glum.

"I miss my mum," said the little one,
Even the bone in its mouth was no fun.
"We will find her soon,"
promised the bigger pup,
Looking hopefully at the shadow coming up.

I told you before 'twas a stormy night,
The puppies were lost in the dark,
with no light in sight.
The ground was covered in frost and snow,
And two little puppies had nowhere to go.

With despair in their eyes,
they snuggled up in a hollow bush,
When the whining wind bought a big *whoosh*!
The wind felt like a bee's sting,
And the pouring rain felt like needles,
dropping from the sky's wing.

Then someone crept in, as quiet as mice,
All wet with snow, cold as ice.
The puppies sat still, without a sound,
When their mother, slowly and gently,
came around.

Autumn
by Keya Patel

Dropping leaves of all kind,
What effect does it have on the mind?
Some think about it as pretty and good,
Some think about it as ugly and bad.
But let us take a moment to think
about its beauty,
As fresh as newly rose, washed with dew.
Just think – what if we have this sight
every day.
To wake up to see bare trees dropping leaves,
of auburn falling on the moist grass below
And to sleep to the sounds of chirruping
birds in the reddening sky,
With the moonlight shining on the bare trees,
it appears to have claws.
But we are told we mustn't yield temptation
to see this enchantment all year.
Instead we must perceive autumn
in all the season.
The season of spring is birth.
Summer is Life.
And winter is slumber.
Autumn is merely a reflection
of these seasons.
Why not do a little something?

Just a little something to help autumn life.
It could even be to value nature,
That cool, crisp, vagrant aroma.
The crunch of the dry, brown leaves.
And the squeak of the slippery,
new yellow leaves.
The shiny bare trees.
All they need is a bit of love
– from you.

Spectacular Space
by Sairithvika Mallina

The gargantuan, fiery-red ball spins through the solar system.
Earth, Jupiter, Saturn, Uranus, Venus, Neptune, Mars, Mercury rotate around,
Passing rutilant rays and a searing heat to each and every planet.
It is like a mighty, sizzling meteor or asteroid gracefully turning around.
Did you know that the ball of molten rock and lava is a luminous star?

The galaxy contained millions and millions of elegant stars, pirouetting around,
like a vibrant, vivid torch beaming through the jet-black midnight sky.
The unique stars were shinier and clearer than a diamond.
Those lavish, luscious gems floated through the solitary sky.
They made a captivating dance by twirling together in unison.

Ominous, ebony-black clouds shrouded the alabaster-white moon.
The thin diamond-white clouds chattered away to each other surreptitiously.
The puffy, orange clouds were like fine, expensive patchwork quilts.
The clouds floated together in the same direction making a soft blanket.
Sometimes the infuriated slate-grey clouds bellowed, making an ear-piercing din.

The moon shone dazzlingly like a distinctive diamond.
It was like a visible, coherent dinner plate that shrouded the sky.

It was an astonishing, spectacular spectacle that could be cherished.

It was a real beauty.

Stars
by Aarav Bibin Bhanu

Oh, bright beautiful stars,
What are you to deceive us all?
You seem only a mile away,
yet you never fall.
Astronauts travel far and wide,
In search of a big bright ball.

Oh, bright beautiful stars,
What will we do without you?
There will be no light in the sky,
No place on earth will be dry.
Spacemen will venture far and wide,
For any sort of immense light.

Oh, bright beautiful stars,
What in the world can we do for you?
You have given us everything,
From impressive lighting,
To pleasure from the king.
What more can we get,
From our brightest things?

We only ask for solar energy,
But I don't think you'll ever be
Brave enough to agree.

Fluffy, My Magic Puppy!
by Adya Gupta Ram

My little pet is such a treat,
It has four cute little paws, a.k.a. feet.
It likes to chase cute cats,
Its fed food with not a lot of fats.
He is tall, handsome and has a face
as charming as a kitten.
It has socks as glittering golden brown
as a mitten.
And... can you believe it? It is magical!
Its calm face is always neutral.
He is MY familiar.
Extraordinary; he can tell the difference
between a truth teller and a liar.
He is a Spark of Brilliance!
Best quality? Hmm... Resilience.
I run with him on his walks,
He encourages me with barks
that makes me feel as if he talks.
His doggy friend's name is Tim,
And my canine friend showed him,
The basket for my doggy friend to sleep,
Because he is such a good dog, I let him keep,
A collar in the shape of a healthy sheep.
Fluffy is my symbol of love, perseverance,
just everything.
I adore my puppy!

My Dream Place
by Harshika Yeleswarapu

My dream place is full of exotic flowers,
Where pretty it always showers.
There are emerald, green, mossy trees,
And a place you will find many bees.

My dream place has wild animals,
You may watch about it on channels.
My dream place you have definitely heard of,
It's where you find not a single white dove.

In my dream place there is colour
in every corner,
There are vines and leaves and trees all over.
There are trees all over, sturdy and stiff,
It smells so tropical, just give a sniff.

You can hear the birds chirping
in the morning,
But there's still the lazy lion's snoring.
My dream place has gone for miles,
To get there it will take a while.

It goes all the way to North-Western Brazil,
If you go that route it will be a tiring drill.
Do you know what it is?
Yes, it's the Amazon rainforest!

Autumn
by Nikola Diakomanolis

The rustling leaves underneath the skinny,
brown trees,
scrunching under people's feet.
Giggling children walking to school,
others think that for school,
they are just too cool.

Trees hibernate as their branches
slowly turn bare,
as there is no more honey
for the poor, poor bears.
Now is a good time for apple pie,
as family gather round
over the gentle autumn sky.

Squirrels start gathering their nut stash.
They find dozens in a flash.

Now everyone is having tons of fun
underneath the autumn sun.

All the way to the moon
by Shon Paul

Speeding along in a rocket ship,
Going as fast as a cheetah,
Flames coming from the back,
All the way to the moon.

Fulfilling my dream,
Seeing all the stars,
As fast as a flash,
All the way to the moon.

Feeling the gravity,
Approaching my destiny,
Whizzing through the planets,
All the way to the moon.

Discovering new things,
Better than Armstrong,
Moving closer and closer,
All the way to the moon.

Breaking all records,
Having a wide smile on my face,
Feeling like a superhero,
All the way to the moon.

Autumn
by Athusga Dineshkumar

September arrives bringing
Yellow, orange and brown
They fall to the ground
Without making a sound.

Autumn is a time filled with enthusiasm
Then September perishes away and brings
lonely October again and September waits
until it comes again.

Later, Halloween comes and goes
The wind is playing autumn games
Through the garden and their lanes
Picking and swirling around.

Apples are crying in their trees trying to be free
The wind is dancing full of fun
Laughing merrily in the sun
Children playing with jollification.

Swallows assemble
And fly to South Africa
Shorter days longer work but
Weather frosty and wet
Get ready for Christmas it is on its way.

Autumn
by Aamna Ahmed

Autumn is a special season,
and I'll tell you why!
When you hear this poem,
You will reach for the sky!

The tall trees drop down leaves.
Yellow, red, orange, purple and brown!
Animals scurry into the bushes.
Hedgehogs, deer, foxes and squirrels!
Autumn flowers, beautiful and bright.
Asher, autumn daffodils and white laceflowers!
The weather mostly changes.
Misty, windy and raining all the time!

Now you know autumn is special,
Leaves colourful and bright!
Wherever it'll be autumn,
You'll say, "What a wonderful sight!"

From the Darkness
by Phoenix Kilgour

As the shadows branch out wide,
Tangling up the sun inside,
Pinpricked stars, they line the heavens.
A pillow for the moon,
As it rests its head on it.
Why must darkness always bring
A fear so harsh, cold and grim?
As the moon rises up high,
The sun lowers down,
Ready to hide.
The darkness of space,
Beautifully laced.
The blackness of the night,
Will help us learn
How we can find the light.
Space is never-ending.
With constellations twisting and bending,
Stars simmering forevermore,
Until they explode with a…

...SUPERNOVA!

Feeling Autumn
by Keera Bates

The leaves are falling, they're calling my name,
all the leaves are never the same,
colourful and bright,
like the stars in the night.

The autumn breeze,
blows leaves off the trees.
In the morning I couldn't see,
the fog was right in front of me.

The pumpkins are spooky,
they give you a scare,
cobwebs are glistening
everywhere.

You know the seasons change every year,
Halloween giving you a spooky cheer.
Some birds fly away to warmer places,
even robins put smiles on our faces.

Hedgehogs hibernating under leaves,
make sure they're not near your bonfire of trees.
The squirrels collect their nuts and seeds,
to make sure they have all they need.

Wrap up warm, with gloves and hats,
look up to the sky and wait for the bats.
Autumn comes but once a year,
so don't be afraid, just give it a cheer!

Autumn
by Hiruki Tennakoon

October, the month when it all starts,
It's the time of year when nature is art.
The cold breeze and susurrus leaves,
The colours of Autumn within the trees.
Leaves of gold falling down,
Floating in the silky air.
They twist and turn like ballerinas,
Before landing here and there.
Squirrels scampering in the twigs,
As swiftly as a fox.
It cunningly hides some conkers,
Among a pile of muddy rocks.
Autumn harvest, collecting food,
Pears and apples, lots to be used.
Pumpkins, corn, from orchard and field,
Giving us our nourishment and daily meals.
Children playing in the golden hue,
Sunset arriving, the day anew.
The day short, the night long,
Now hibernating creatures come along.
Bears, bats, snakes and bees,
They all start to begin their deep sleep.

Dying to live a many more
by Rosy Ilieva

Bury me in the floors of mother nature
that I may die to live
close with my family
I shall spring forth
a new refreshed, happy soul
dwelling on the earth
full of nourishment and joyfulness
I am fully mature and full of confidence
I will dwell in my food and drink
In it everyone will find a legion of me
I will feed any hungry children
I will giver shelter for any shivering people.

Maybe a beauty for a home or two
or medicine for the infected
oh lord
do keep me alive
bury me many times
so I can live many more
and help many more people.

Autumn
by Bumiga Barathethas

The crisp air and the cool breeze,
You hear amber and gold leaves,
rustling about on the trees.

A shimmering sun watching silently from above,
Sending an abundance of her love.

A leaf flies away from each tree,
like an inelegant bird,
Seeing them drop one by one
without a sound to be heard.

The invigorating smell of fresh air,
Embracing you as if it does really care.

The bitter taste of dry earth,
Anyone there might feel a sense of mirth.

At how tranquil and serene it is,
You would feel like you'd just won a quiz.

Clear and cloudless is the azure sky,
Not yet time to say goodbye.

As you trample over the damp grass,
Autumn must have to pass.

Rain showers over the towering trees,
So chilly that you could freeze.

All is quiet but the sound of drizzle,
As the leaves curl up and shrivel.

The sky is a spectator as it stares at the setting,
The more windier and colder it is getting.

It stops raining after a while,
After having rained with as much water
as in the Nile.

Autumn is such a lovely season,
Though some might not know the reason.

The Solar System and Space
by Kayla Osileye

As the glimmering stars shine bright in the night
Rocket ships quickly take flight
All eight planets stay upright
Except Uranus that turns and sits on its side
While Mercury is the hottest
and closest to the sun
Beautiful Venus is
the morning and evening star
Our Earth's the planet we live on today
Though Mars we could live on
but not in many ways
Jupiter is the biggest planet in our solar system
While Saturn is like a balloon
and stands out with ringlets
Still Uranus sits quietly on its side
While Neptune is the smallest
and has no gases inside
Finally there's Pluto and it's the dwarf planet
That sits in the dark with the blue sky
and red snow

The solar system's planets
keep on moving and moving
And their moons go around them
spinning and spinning
While we do not notice
our planet Earth spins around us
Our moon spins and spins above us
White holes and Black holes
are on the rush to form
Then the hot bright sun burns them off
and oh what a storm
When I look at the sky and stars in the night
I realise the beauty of life on Earth
Then I sit up and start to think
Oh how lovely it would be to see the stars
and sky from another planet

Flowers
by Joanna Idowu

Flowers, flowers,
growing tall like towers.

It grows summer, spring
or in the evening.

As they sprout out from the ground,
each other they surround.

Their glowing beauty in the sun,
all unique each one.

The bright colours and sweet smells,
leaves a wonderful aroma wherever it dwells.

As the scent travels through the air,
it brings such joy instead of despair.

As the season comes to an end,
new flowers will grow again.

Acknowledgements & Sponsors

I would like to thank my team, Olivia Eisinger and Zara Thatcher, for their commitment and work ethic to our first Spark of Brilliance Poetry Competition and book.

Next, I would like to acknowledge the judges – Dexter Moscow, Alice Merry, David Lakey, Zara Thatcher and Olivia Eisinger – who freely gave of their time to help us get to the point of choosing 30 poems.

I want to thank Tammy Clark for speaking about 'daring to dream' and for so generously using her talents to design the front cover of *Spark of Brilliance, Volume 1*.

A big thank you to our printers, 4edge Ltd, particularly Carl, who have sponsored the printing of the copies for each of the 30 finalists.

Thank you also goes to John Turner, CEO of Simply Business Design and Founder of Educational Life CIC, for his support and sponsorship as well as compèring the Grand Final of Spark of Brilliance.

Thank you to Lady Waynett Peters for handing the prizes at our Grand Final.

I want to acknowledge the schools who encouraged the children to participate in the poetry competition and would like to thank them for their dedication and the great job that they do for our future voices.

Well done to all of the winners who attended the Spark of Brilliance Grand Final at Bourne Hall.

Thank you to the staff of Bourne Hall in Ewell, Surrey for all their efforts in preparing the venue and making the day memorable.

Lastly, but not least, I want to thank all of the children who entered the competition. As we all know, it is the taking part that counts most of all.

Brenda Dempsey
CEO
Book Brilliance Publishing